Stephen Savage

This edition published in 2014 by Wayland
Copyright © Wayland 2014

Wayland
338 Euston Road
London NW1 3BH

Wayland Australia
Level 17/207 Kent Street
Sydney, NSW 2000

Editor: Carron Brown
Designer: Alyssa Peacock

Dewey number: 598-dc23

ISBN 978 0 7502 7992 5

Printed in China

10 9 8 7 6 5 4 3 2 1

Picture acknowledgements: Andrew Purcell 4, /Scott Nielson 6, /Mike McKavett 7(l), /Tea Maeklong 7(r), /Paolo Fioratti 8(t), /Kim Taylor 8(b), /Leonard Lee Rue 9, 11, /Gordon Langsbury 14(t), /Wayne Lankinen 17(t), /C. & D. Frith 18, /Andre Anita 20, /Patryk Kosmider 21(b), /George McCarthy 22(b), /John Markham 22 (b inset), /Eckart Pott 23, 26, /Kim Taylor 25(l), /John Cancalosi 25(r) and title page (r), /Marie Read 27; FLPA / Bob Langrish 19; Jaja/Shutterstock.com 5, /Stephen Dalton 10(t) and contents page, /John Shaw 10(b) and title page, /N.R. Coulton 12, /Stephen Dalton 13(t), /B. & C. Alexander 13(b), /Alan Williams 14(b), /Vincente Canseco 15, /Natalia Paklina 16, /Gerard Lacz 17, /Rich Kirchner 22(t); Oxford Scientific Films © Heinz Schrempp/Okapia 24; Judy Whitton/Shutterstock.com, cover picture; Wayland Picture Library 21(b).

First published in 2000 by Wayland

Wayland is a division of Hachette Children's Books, an Hachette UK company.
www.hachette.co.uk

# Contents

# What a difference!

The main difference between birds and most other animals is that birds can fly.

## BIRD CHARACTERISTICS

- Birds are warm-blooded.
- Their bodies are covered in feathers.
- They have two wings.
- They use a bill to obtain food.
- They lay eggs to produce young.

The ostrich is ➡ the world's largest bird. Ostriches cannot fly because they are too heavy, sometimes weighing up to 156 kilograms (345 pounds).

Birds can be very different from each other. Some are large; others are tiny. Many birds have unusual bills. Some have brilliantly coloured feathers.

The male bird of paradise has ➔ brightly coloured feathers to attract a female.

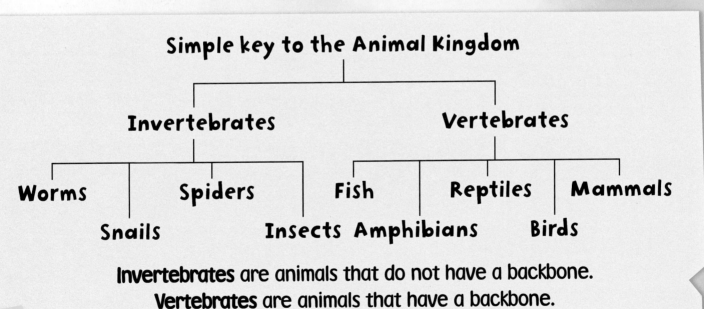

## Simple key to the Animal Kingdom

Invertebrates                    Vertebrates

Worms          Spiders      Fish      Reptiles   Mammals
     Snails           Insects  Amphibians     Birds

**Invertebrates** are animals that do not have a backbone.
**Vertebrates** are animals that have a backbone.

# Where birds live

Birds live in all of the world's habitats, including forests, grasslands, deserts, seashores, mountains, lakes, rivers and on the sea. Some even live in polar regions.

## LIVING IN DIFFERENT HABITATS

- Forest and woodland birds have clawed feet for gripping branches.
- Ducks have webbed feet for swimming.
- Birds that live in water have waterproof feathers.
- Vultures have large wings for gliding over grassland.

← Snowy owls live in the frozen Arctic. Their white feathers keep them warm and camouflaged against the snow.

Birds have special features that help them live in these very different habitats. These features include long legs, webbed and clawed feet, and bills of different shapes.

← The tree creeper has large, clawed feet for gripping bark. Its bill is curved for poking into holes in search of insects.

↑ This stilt has long legs for wading in shallow water and a long bill so it can reach food on the lake bottom.

# Catching a meal

The shape of a bird's bill, or beak, is a clue to the type of food it eats. Eagles have sharp beaks for tearing food into bite-sized pieces.

Parrots and finches use their strong beaks to crack open seeds and nuts or to scoop out fruit. A thin bill is good for catching insects.

↑ The kingfisher dives into the river to catch small fish.

← The pied wagtail eats insects that it catches on the ground or in the air.

⬆ A parrot can hold a nut in its foot while breaking the shell with its tough beak.

Hawks and eagles have excellent eyesight to spot small mammals. They dive on their prey, grabbing it with their clawed feet.

← A bald eagle searches the ground, looking for prey.

↓ A peregrine falcon eats other, smaller birds, which it may catch on the ground or in the air.

A few birds use tools to catch food. The woodpecker finch holds a cactus spine in its beak to pull insects from holes in trees. The Egyptian vulture picks up stones with its beak and drops them onto ostrich eggs to break the shells.

Vultures feed on → dead animals.

## AVOIDING PREDATORS

- Female birds are often brown, so they cannot be spotted on their nests easily.

- The fulmar can spit foul liquid at an attacker.

- Ducks and swans often sleep on water, where they are safe from attack.

# Hot and cold

Birds have soft, fluffy feathers to keep them warm. They must bathe regularly, even in winter, to keep their feathers clean.

Some birds fly to warmer regions in the winter and return the following year. This is called migration.

⬆ Many birds have a patch of bare skin on their breast. This mallard uses its body warmth to keep its eggs warm.

← Swallows breed in Europe and North America. In the winter they migrate south to warmer regions. This swallow is drinking as it flies over a river.

↓ A thick layer of blubber and tightly packed feathers keep emperor penguins warm in the frozen Antarctic.

↑ Arctic terns fly about 35,000 kilometres (22,000 miles) to migrate to warmer climates.

This bee-eater is 'gaping' to cool → itself. It may die if it gets too hot.

**A bird cannot sweat to lose body heat as most mammals do. It can cool itself by sitting with its bill open, 'gaping'.**

Birds that live in deserts and other very hot regions rest in the shade during the hottest part of the day.

↓ A heron spreads its wings to cast a shadow over the nest to keep the eggs cool.

# Getting around

Most birds use their wings to fly. When a bird flaps its wings, the flight feathers in the wings push against the air. This lifts the bird off the ground and pushes it forwards.

⬇ The wings of a wandering albatross measure 3.3 metres (11 feet) from the tip of one to the tip of the other. The albatross can glide for hours without flapping its wings.

A hummingbird → hovers by beating its wings 70 times a second. It needs to hover so that it can sip nectar from flowers.

**Small birds have short wings that they must flap very quickly.**
**Birds with larger wings flap slowly and can glide to save their energy.**

↓ Penguins use their flipper-like wings to swim underwater.

The double-wattled → cassowary cannot fly. It escapes predators by running. It can also swim across rivers.

## WAYS OF MOVING

- Birds that fly have lightweight bones.
- A bird uses its tail for steering.
- Emperor penguins toboggan along the snow on their stomachs.
- Mute swans run along the water to take off.
- The flightless ostrich can run at 70 kilometres per hour (40 miles per hour).
- Swifts spend most of their life in the air, including sleeping in short naps.

There are about 40 types of birds that cannot fly. Many of these have developed large, powerful legs for running.

Flightless birds may have lost the ability to fly because they no longer needed to fly to find food or escape from danger.

↓ The roadrunner rarely flies. It uses its wings for balance to run after prey at up to 40 kilometres per hour (26 miles per hour).

# Hatching and raising chicks

Male and female birds come together to breed and raise their young. Some birds sing a courtship song to attract a mate. Others perform a complicated dance.

↓ These Japanese red crowned cranes are performing a courtship dance. They will probably stay together for life.

↑ A female blackbird brings food for her young. The chicks are hatched with few feathers, so they cannot fly.

## Most birds lay their eggs in a nest. This may be a simple pile of twigs or a neat, carefully woven nest.

Young swans, called cygnets, follow their ➡ parents soon after hatching. The adult swans teach the cygnets how to survive.

← Plovers nest on the ground. This golden plover pretends it has a broken wing to lure a predator away from its nest.

There are many predators on the lookout for eggs or chicks. Parent birds have to keep a constant watch and will fight off raiders.

↓ Cuckoos lay their eggs in other birds' nests (inset). This little reed warbler is trying to feed the huge cuckoo chick it has raised.

## UNUSUAL NESTING PLACES

- Some types of penguins nest in old rabbit burrows.
- The male parent emperor penguin looks after the egg while the female feeds in the sea. He balances the egg on his feet to keep it off the snow.
- European wrens may nest in garden sheds.
- Mallards sometimes nest in hollow trees.

↓ White storks often build their nests on high rooftops, such as churches.

Some birds nest in large colonies, making it harder for predators to attack. However, squabbles often break out among neighbours.

# Pet birds

## CARING FOR PET BIRDS

- Make sure your cage has plenty of space.
- Provide the correct food and water.
- Remember that birds kept on their own need human company.
- Many birds enjoy a spray of fine water.
- Provide a supply of food and water in the garden for wild birds, especially during cold weather.

Birds are often kept as pets, but they need special care. You can study the characteristics of birds by looking closely at pet birds.

Pet parakeets ➡ should be kept in a cage with plenty of space or in an outdoor aviary. In the wild they live in large flocks.

Birds need to fly. When they are young, they can be trained to fly around the room and then return to their cage.

↓ A bird feeder with nuts will attract wild birds, such as these great and blue tits, to visit your garden.

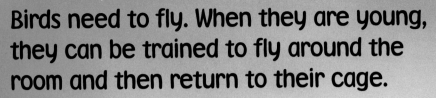

Cockatoos make good pets. → Like parakeets, they should have plenty of space and company. Pet cockatoos can mimic human words.

# Unusual birds

Many birds have special features that help them survive. For instance, owls have extra-large eyes to help them see in the dark.

↓ The secretary bird looks like an eagle on stilts. It kills large prey, such as snakes, by stamping on them.

Some birds have unusual habits. Oxpeckers ride on the backs of large, grass-eating animals. They feed on the parasites and flies living on the animals' skin, helping to clean the animals at the same time.

↑ Pelicans plunge their heads underwater, catching fish in their net-like beaks.

## UNUSUAL FEATURES

- Pelicans have a beak pouch to store fish.
- A sword-billed hummingbird's bill is as long as its body.
- Hoatzin chicks have claws on their wings for climbing trees in their rainforest home.

# Scale of birds

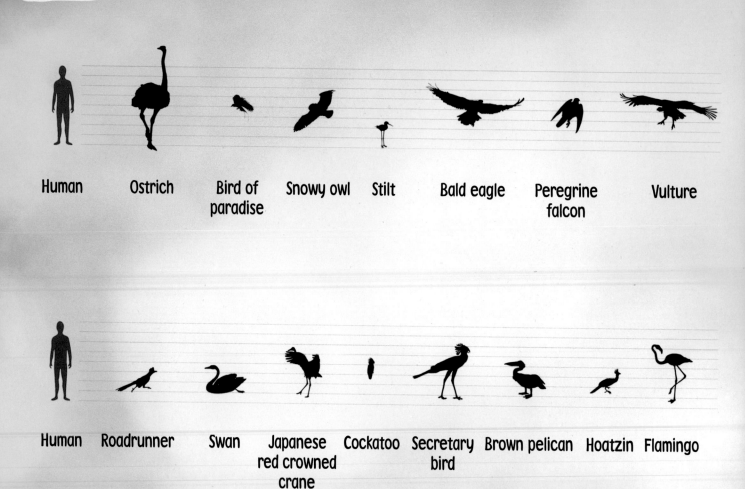

Human    Ostrich    Bird of paradise    Snowy owl    Stilt    Bald eagle    Peregrine falcon    Vulture

Human    Roadrunner    Swan    Japanese red crowned crane    Cockatoo    Secretary bird    Brown pelican    Hoatzin    Flamingo

Human    Fulmar    Mallard    Emperor penguin    Arctic tern    Heron    Black-necked stork    Wandering albatross    Double-wattled cassowary

Bee-eater    Hummingbird    Swift    Blackbird    Golden plover    Human hand

Tree creeper    Kingfisher    Pied wagtail    African grey parrot    Swallow    Human hand

Cuckoo    Reed warbler    Parakeet    Oxpecker    Woodpecker wren    Wren    Human hand

# Index

Page numbers in **bold** refer to photographs.